Oh! My SPEAKING 2

CEDU BOOK

UNIT COMPONENTS

• KEY PATTERNS

Key words and key patterns are presented in context.
Students can role-play the conversation used in the cartoon.

• VOCABULARY

Vocabulary words can be used immediately through activities related to pattern sentences.

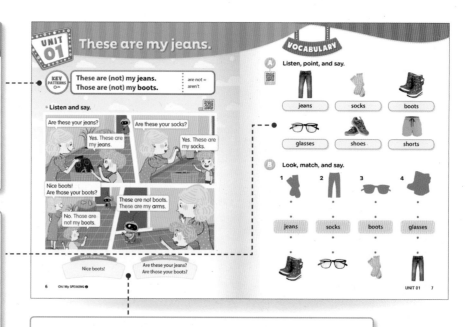

• USEFUL EXPRESSIONS & QUESTIONS

A variety of particularly useful expressions from the dialogues in the cartoons allow students to develop their speaking skills.

• KEY PATTERN PRACTICE

Repeating sentences with key patterns helps students to naturally remember what they have learned.

• LISTEN AND SPEAK

Substituting words in key patterns in a combined listening and speaking activity assists students to build their speaking fluency.

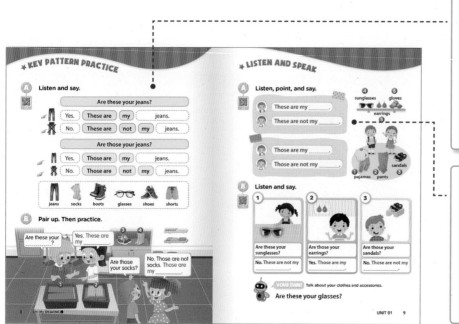

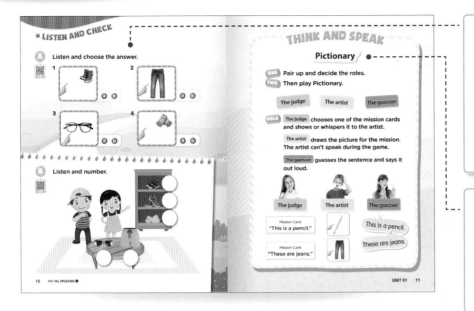

Listen and choose the answer.

THINK AND SPEAK

Pictionary

ONE Pair up and decide the roles.

TWO Then play Pictionary.

The judge   The artist   The guesser

ROLE The judge chooses one of the mission cards and shows or whispers it to the artist.

The artist draws the picture for the mission. The artist can't speak during the game.

The guesser guesses the sentence and says it out loud.

The judge   The artist   The guesser

Mission Card "This is a pencil."

Mission Card "These are jeans."

This is a pencil.

These are jeans.

Listen and number.

• LISTEN AND CHECK

Listening practice gets students to relate the key sentences to the pictures and to learn how to use the right sentences in the conversation.

• THINK AND SPEAK

A fun and educational communication game gets students to practice key sentences repeatedly.

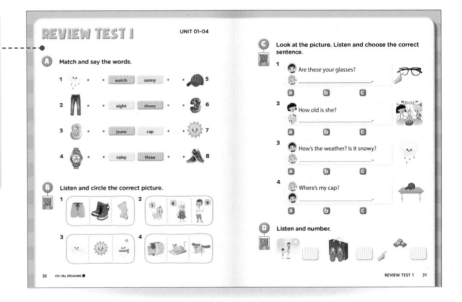

REVIEW TEST

Word reviews and a variety of speaking and listening activities help students recall and further practice key words and key patterns from previous units.

REVIEW TEST I   UNIT 01-04

A Match and say the words.

1 watch sunny 5
2 eight shoes 6
3 jeans cap 7
4 rainy three 8

B Listen and circle the correct picture.

C Look at the picture. Listen and choose the correct sentence.

1 Are these your glasses?
   a   b   c

2 How old is she?
   a   b   c

3 How's the weather? Is it snowy?
   a   b   c

4 Where's my cap?
   a   b   c

D Listen and number.

WORKBOOK

Various writing, listening, and speaking exercises allow students to review key words and key patterns learned in the Student Book.

CONTENTS

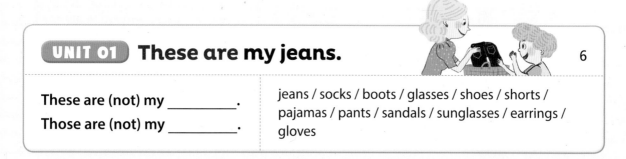

UNIT 01

These are my jeans.

KEY PATTERNS

These are (not) my jeans.
Those are (not) my boots.

are not = aren't

Listen and say.

Are these your jeans?

Yes. These are my jeans.

Are these your socks?

Yes. These are my socks.

Nice boots!
Are those your boots?

These are not boots.
These are my arms.

No. Those are not my boots.

Useful Expression

Nice boots!

Useful Questions

Are these your jeans?
Are those your boots?

A Listen, point, and say.

jeans

socks

boots

glasses

shoes

shorts

B Look, match, and say.

1

2

3

4

jeans

socks

boots

glasses

★ KEY PATTERN PRACTICE

A Listen and say.

	Are these your jeans?			
	Yes.	These are	my	jeans.
	No.	These are	not	my	jeans.

	Are those your jeans?			
	Yes.	Those are	my	jeans.
	No.	Those are	not	my	jeans.

 jeans   socks   boots   glasses   shoes   shorts

B Pair up. Then practice.

Are these your _____?

Yes. These are my _____.

Are those your socks?

No. Those are not socks. Those are my _____.

⭐ LISTEN AND SPEAK

 A **Listen, point, and say.**

These are my _____.

These are not my _____.

Those are my _____.

Those are not my _____.

④ sunglasses　⑥ gloves

earrings
⑤

① pajamas　② pants　③ sandals

 B **Listen and say.**

1

Are these your sunglasses?

No. These are not my _____.

2

Are those your earrings?

Yes. Those are my _____.

3

Are those your sandals?

No. Those are not my _____.

 **YOUR TURN!** Talk about your clothes and accessories.

Are these your glasses?

★ LISTEN AND CHECK

A Listen and choose the answer.

1

a b

2

a b

3

a b

4

a b

B Listen and number.

THINK AND SPEAK

Pictionary

ONE Pair up and decide the roles.

TWO Then play Pictionary.

The judge   The artist   The guesser

ROLE The judge chooses one of the mission cards and shows or whispers it to the artist.

The artist draws the picture for the mission. The artist can't speak during the game.

The guesser guesses the sentence and says it out loud.

The judge

The artist

The guesser

Mission Card
"This is a pencil."

This is a pencil.

Mission Card
"These are jeans."

These are jeans.

UNIT 02
I'm eight years old.

I'm eight years old.
She's five years old.

I'm = I am
She's = She is

Listen and say.

Wacky, this is Amy. Amy, this is Wacky.

Nice to meet you.

Nice to meet you, too.

I'm eight years old. How old are you, Amy?

I'm eight years old, too. Wacky, how old are you?

I'm one year old.

This is my little sister. She's five years old.

Oh, you're a baby.

No! I'm not a baby. I'm a robot.

Useful Expression

Wacky, this is Amy.

Useful Question

How old are you?

A Listen, point, and say.

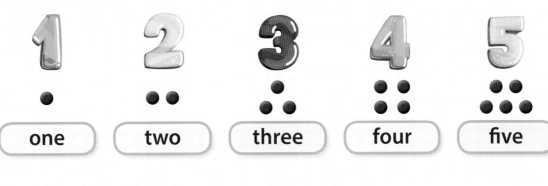

| one | two | three | four | five |

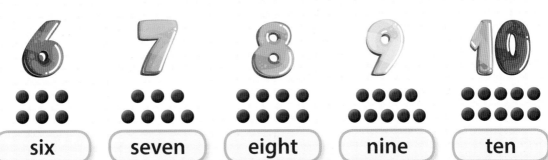

| six | seven | eight | nine | ten |

B Count, match, and say.

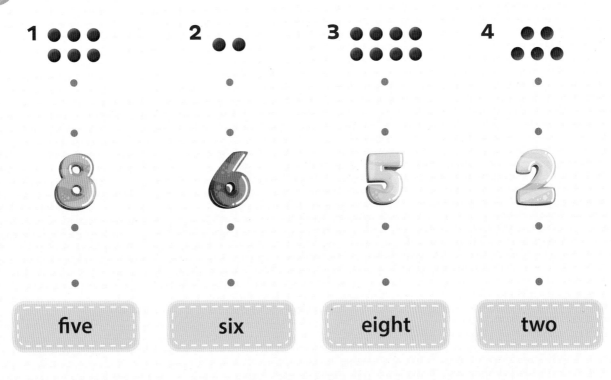

1   2   3   4

| five | six | eight | two |

⋆ KEY PATTERN PRACTICE

A Listen and say.

8 How old are you?	How old is he/she?
I'm	eight	**year(s) old.**	**He's She's**	eight	**year(s) old.**

1 one	**2** two	**3** three	**4** four	**5** five
6 six	**7** seven	**8** eight	**9** nine	**10** ten

B Pair up. Then practice.

How old is he/she?

I'm 10 years old.

I'm 7 years old.

He's/She's _____ years old.

I'm 5 years old.

1 brother **2** sister **3** cousin

★ LISTEN AND SPEAK

A Listen, point, and say.

 How old are you?

 I'm ____ years old.

 How old is he/she?

 He's/She's ____ years old.

11 eleven   **12** twelve   **13** thirteen   **14** fourteen   **15** fifteen

16 sixteen   **17** seventeen   **18** eighteen   **19** nineteen   **20** twenty

B Listen and say.

1 How old are you?

I'm _____ years old.

2 How old is he?

He's _____ years old.

 **YOUR TURN!** Ask and answer your friends.

How old are you?

★ LISTEN AND CHECK

A Listen and circle.

1

2

3

4

B Listen and choose the answer.

1

2

3

THINK AND SPEAK

Bingo!

ONE Randomly write numbers from 1 to 20.

TWO Pair up. Take turns to call out the numbers in the sentence, "I'm _____."

THREE The first student to either get a line or full house has to call out "Bingo!"

I'm <u>one</u>.

I'm <u>twenty</u>.

		20	
	1		

It's cold.

Is it cold?
It's (not) cold.

It's = It is

Listen and say.

How's the weather?

It's windy.

Is it cold?

No. It's not cold.

Look! There's Amy.

Let's go outside.

Achoo! Excuse me.

Sorry! It's so cold.
Let's go inside.

Useful Expressions

Excuse me.
Let's go outside/inside.

Useful Question

How's the weather?

VOCABULARY

Listen, point, and say.

windy   sunny   snowy

rainy   foggy   cold   hot

B

Look, match, and say.

1
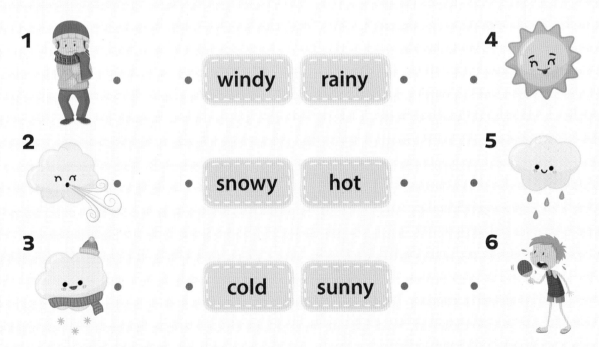

windy   rainy

2

snowy   hot

3

cold   sunny

4

5

6

⭐ KEY PATTERN PRACTICE

A Listen and say.

Is **it** windy?

Yes. **It's** windy.

No. **It's** **not** windy.

windy	sunny	snowy	rainy	foggy	cold	hot

B Pair up. Then practice.

① ②

③ ④

Is it _____?   Yes. It's _____.

Is it _____?   No. It's not _____.
It's foggy.

⭐ LISTEN AND SPEAK

A Listen, point, and say.

Is it _____ ?

Yes. It's _____ .

No. It's not _____ .

cloudy

stormy

dry

warm

cool

B Listen and say.

1

Is it cool?

Yes. It's _____ .

2

Is it stormy?

No. It's not _____ .
It's _____ .

3

Is it dry?

Yes. It's _____ .

YOUR TURN! Talk about today's weather.

How's the weather today?

A Listen and match.

1  2  3  4

B Listen and number.

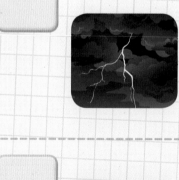

THINK AND SPEAK

Role-Play

ONE Look at the weather in each picture and fill in the blanks.

TWO Then role-play.

rainy   windy   sunny

It's in the bag.

KEY PATTERNS

It's in the bag.
They're under the bed.
They're on your head!

It's = It is
They're = They are

Listen and say.

Where's my watch?

It's in the bag.

Where are my slippers?

They're under the bed.

Oh, here they are. Thanks, Wacky.

You're welcome.

Where are my sunglasses? They're not in the bag.

They're on your head!

Useful Expression

Here they are.

Useful Questions

Where's my watch?
Where are my slippers?

A Listen, point, and say.

watch   cap   slippers   mittens

in   on   under

B Listen, number, and say.

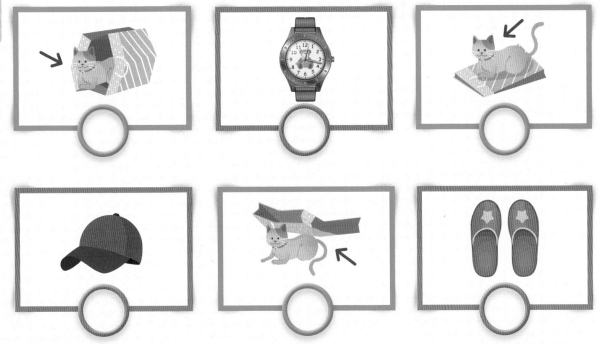

⭐ KEY PATTERN PRACTICE

A **Listen and say.**

| **Where's my watch?** | **Where are my slippers?** |

It's **in** the bag. **They're** **under** the bag.

watch   cap   slippers   mittens   in   on   under

B **Pair up. Then practice.**

Where are my _____?

Where's my _____?

It's _____ the bag.

They're _____ the bag.

★ LISTEN AND SPEAK

A Listen, point, and say.

 Where's my _____?

It's _____ the bag.

Where are my _____?

They're _____ the bag.

1 belt

2 umbrella

3 rain boots

4 earphones

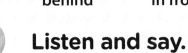

behind   in front of   next to

B Listen and say.

1

Where are my rain boots?

They're _____.

2

Where's my umbrella?

It's _____.

3

Where's my belt?

It's _____.

YOUR TURN! Ask and answer your friends.

Where's my cap?

⭐ LISTEN AND CHECK

A Listen and check.

1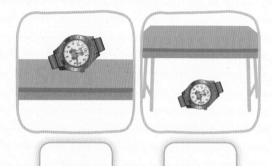

2

3

4

B Listen and number.

THINK AND SPEAK

Show and Tell

ONE Pair up. Each student draws some of these things in different locations in the picture.

TWO First, one student asks questions. Then, the other student answers while looking at the drawing. Switch roles.

Where's my cap?

It's on the bag.

Where are my slippers?

They're under the desk.

REVIEW TEST 1

A Match and say the words.

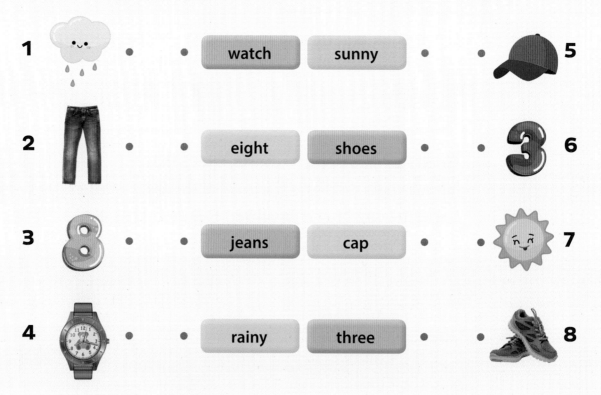

1 • • watch sunny • • 5

2 • • eight shoes • • 6

3 • • jeans cap • • 7

4 • • rainy three • • 8

B Listen and circle the correct picture.

1

2

3

4

C Look at the picture. Listen and choose the correct sentence.

1

Are these your glasses?

_____.

a   b   c

2

How old is she?

_____.

a   b   c

3

How's the weather? Is it snowy?

_____.

a   b   c

4

Where's my cap?

_____.

a   b   c

D Listen and number.

E Talk about the weather.

STEP 1 Choose and write the correct sentence for each blank.

That's my cap

It's sunny

These are my shorts

How's the weather?

_____.

Is this your cap?

Yes. _____.

Are those your shorts?

Yes. _____.

STEP 2 Draw today's weather and your clothes.
Then write about your picture.

It's _____.

This is my _____.

 These are my _____.

UNIT 05

I like donuts.

KEY PATTERNS

I like **donuts.**
I don't like **donuts.**

don't =
do not

Listen and say.

33

I like donuts.
Do you like donuts?

No. I don't like donuts.

I like kiwis.
Do you like kiwis?

No. I don't like kiwis.

Then what do you like?

Well…

I don't like food.
I don't eat food.
Plug me in, please.

Oh, I see. Okay!

Useful Expression

Plug me in, please.

Useful Questions

Do you like donuts?
What do you like?

A Listen, point, and say.

apples	kiwis	grapes

donuts	hamburgers	sandwiches

B Look, match, and say.

1 •

4 •

hamburgers   kiwis

2 •

5 •

grapes   apples

3 •

6 •

donuts   sandwiches

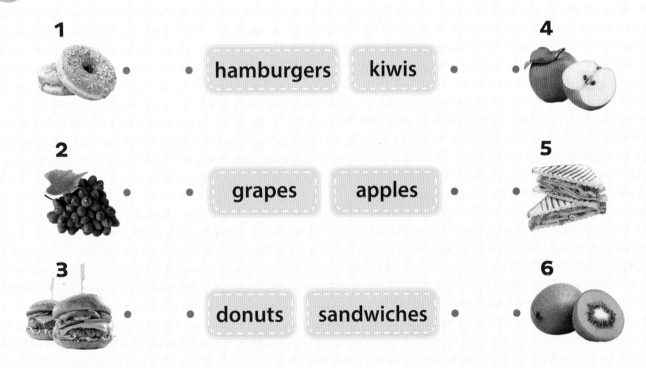

✦ KEY PATTERN PRACTICE

A **Listen and say.**

> **Do you like apples?**

Yes. | I | like | apples.

No. | I | don't | like | apples.

apples kiwis grapes donuts hamburgers sandwiches

B **Pair up. Then practice.**

I like _____.
Do you like _____ ?

Yes. I like _____.

No. I don't like _____.
I like pizza.

1   2   3

LISTEN AND SPEAK

A Listen, point, and say.

Do you like _____?

Yes. I like _____.

No. I don't like _____.

1 bananas

2 oranges

3 watermelons

4 ice cream

5 cheese

6 pizza

B Listen and say.

1

I like ice cream.
Do you like ice cream?

Yes. I like _____.

2

Do you like oranges?

No. I don't like _____.

I like _____.

YOUR TURN! Talk about the food that you like.

Do you like apples?

★ LISTEN AND CHECK

A Listen and match.

 1   2    3    4

B Listen and number.

Class Survey

ONE Draw and write two more items.

TWO Ask your friends about the food.
Write O in the box if they like the food,
or X in the box if they don't like the food.

 Do you like <u>bananas</u>?

Yes. I like <u>bananas</u>.

No. I don't like <u>bananas</u>.

Friend's Name	bananas	apples	oranges	-----------	-----------

UNIT 06

Does she like tomatoes?

KEY PATTERNS

Does she like tomatoes?
She likes cucumbers.
She doesn't like tomatoes.

doesn't =
does not

• Listen and say.

Let's make breakfast for Mom.

Okay.

Does she like vegetables?

Yes. She likes cucumbers and potatoes.

I see. Does she like tomatoes?

No. She doesn't like tomatoes, but she likes tomato ketchup.

Okay. Let's put in tomato ketchup.

Oh no! That's too much!

Useful Expression

That's too much!

Useful Question

Does she like vegetables?

VOCABULARY

A Listen, point, and say.

cucumbers

onions

tomatoes

carrots

potatoes

pumpkins

B Listen, number, and say.

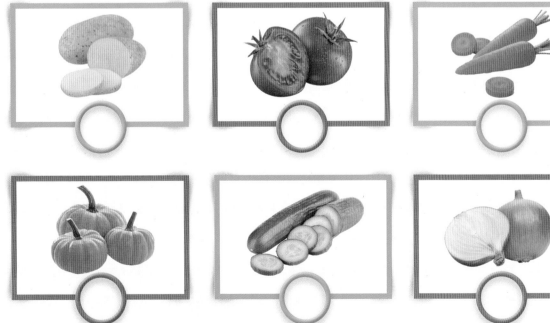

★ KEY PATTERN PRACTICE

A Listen and say.

| Does | he/she | like | cucumbers? |

Yes. | He/She | likes | cucumbers.

No. | He/She | doesn't | like | cucumbers.

cucumbers   onions   tomatoes   carrots   potatoes   pumpkins

B Pair up. Then practice.

Let's make breakfast for Mom. Does she like _____?

Yes. She likes _____.

No. She doesn't like _____. She likes carrots.

★ LISTEN AND SPEAK

A Listen, point, and say.

Does he/she like _____?

Yes. He/She likes _____.

No. He/She doesn't like _____.

1 sweet potatoes

2 mushrooms

3 green peas

4 eggplants

5 broccoli

6 cabbages

B Listen and ask.

1

Does he like _____?

Yes. He likes **sweet potatoes**.

2

Does she like _____?

No. She doesn't like **broccoli**. She likes **cabbages**.

YOUR TURN! Talk about the vegetables that your mom and dad like.

Does she like vegetables?

★ LISTEN AND CHECK

A Listen and choose the answer.

46

1 　2 　3

ⓐ　　ⓑ　　　ⓐ　　ⓑ　　　ⓐ　　ⓑ

B Listen and number.

47

Making a Shopping List

ONE Make a vegetable pizza for your friend.

TWO Ask your partner about vegetables and check the ones he/she likes in the box.

Do you like <u>carrots</u>?

Yes. I like <u>carrots</u>.
No. I don't like <u>carrots</u>.

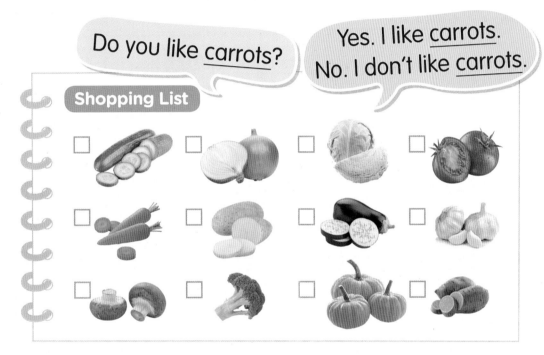

Shopping List

THREE Present it in front of the class.

Let's make a vegetable pizza for my friend.

Good idea. Does he/she like <u>potatoes</u>?

Yes. He/She likes <u>potatoes</u>, but he/she doesn't like <u>sweet potatoes</u>.

I see.

Do you have a bike?

KEY PATTERNS

Do you have a bike?
I have a bike.
I don't have a bike.

don't =
do not

Listen and say.

Useful Expressions

Happy birthday.
These are for you.

Useful Question

Do you have a skateboard?

A Listen, point, and say.

a bike

a skateboard

a scooter

a soccer ball

a bat

a racket

B Follow and say.

1

2

3

4

a bike   a soccer ball   a racket   a skateboard

★ KEY PATTERN PRACTICE

A Listen and say.

| Do | you | have | a bike? |

Yes. | I | have | a bike.

No. | I | don't | have | a bike.

a bike   a skateboard   a scooter   a soccer ball   a bat   a racket

B Pair up. Then practice.

Do you have _____?

Yes. I have _____.

No. I don't have _____, but I have a bike.

★ LISTEN AND SPEAK

A Listen, point, and say.

Do you have _____ ?

Yes. I have _____ .

No. I don't have _____ .

① a baseball

② a basketball

③ a tennis ball

④ a sled

⑤ a snowboard

⑥ inline skates

⑦ ice skates

B Listen and say.

1

Do you have a baseball?

No. I don't have _____ ,
but I have _____ .

2

Do you have inline skates?

Yes. I have _____ .

YOUR TURN! Talk about the sports equipment that you have.

Do you have a bike?

★ LISTEN AND CHECK

A Listen and match.

1  2  3 4

B Listen and number.

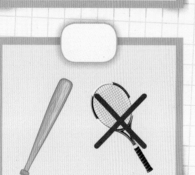 

THINK AND SPEAK

Pick and Take

ONE Prepare 2 card sets for a pair or a team. Place 1 set face down in front of the dealer.

(One person is the dealer and the rest are the players.)

TWO Each player is given the same number of cards.

THREE The dealer picks a card and asks one player "Do you have _____?" to find a match.

FOUR If that person has the card, the dealer owns the card. If not, the next person becomes the dealer.

FIVE Whoever gains the most cards wins the game.

Do you have <u>a bike</u>?

dealer

Yes. I have <u>a bike</u>.
(Give *a bike* card to the dealer.)

No. I don't have <u>a bike</u>.
(I'm the dealer now.)

UNIT 08

He has big ears.

KEY PATTERNS

Does he have big eyes?
He has big ears.
He doesn't have big eyes.

doesn't =
does not

Listen and say.

 55

Are you drawing Jack?

Yes. Jack has big ears.

You're right. He has big ears.

Does he have big eyes?

No. He doesn't have big eyes. He has small eyes.

He has a long tail.

What? I don't have a tail!

He doesn't have a tail!

It's a cat.

She has a long tail.

Useful Expression

You're right.

Useful Question

Are you drawing Jack?

VOCABULARY

A Listen, point, and say.

a nose

a mouth

eyes

ears

hands

feet

B Look, match, and say.

1

2

3

4

a mouth

a nose

feet

eyes

★ KEY PATTERN PRACTICE

A Listen and say.

| Does | he/she | have | a big nose**?** |

 Yes. **He/She** **has** a big nose.

 No. **He/She** **doesn't** **have** a big nose.

big ⟷ small

 a nose   a mouth eyes ears hands feet

B Pair up. Then practice.

Does he have a big _____?

Does she have big _____?

Yes. He has a big _____.

No. She doesn't have big _____.
She has small _____.

⭐ LISTEN AND SPEAK

A Listen, point, and say.

Does he/she have (a) long _____?

Yes. He/She has (a) long _____.

No. He/She doesn't have (a) long _____.

long ⟷ short

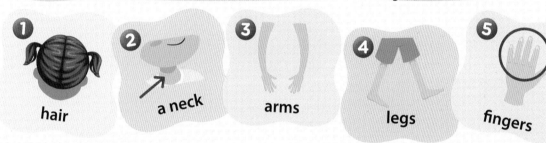

1. hair
2. a neck
3. arms
4. legs
5. fingers

B Listen and say.

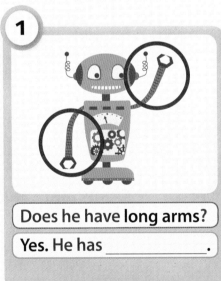

1

Does he have **long arms?**

Yes. He has _____.

2

Does she have **a long neck?**

No. She doesn't have _____.
She has _____.

YOUR TURN! Describe your friend's body parts.

Does he have a big nose?

★ LISTEN AND CHECK

A Listen and match.

1
2
3
4

B Listen and number.

Making a Monster

ONE Prepare two dice. The first die has the body parts and the second die has the numbers 1 to 3 and the adjectives, *big*, *short*, and *long*.

TWO Roll the second die twice, the first time to pick a number, then the second time to pick an adjective. Combine the three items to make a sentence.

(Rolling the body part die) eye(s)
(Rolling the number & adjective die)
three and big

(Drawing a monster)
He has <u>three big eyes</u>…

My monster has <u>three big eyes</u>.

He has _____.

He has _____.

He has _____.

He doesn't have _____.

REVIEW TEST 2

A Match and say the words.

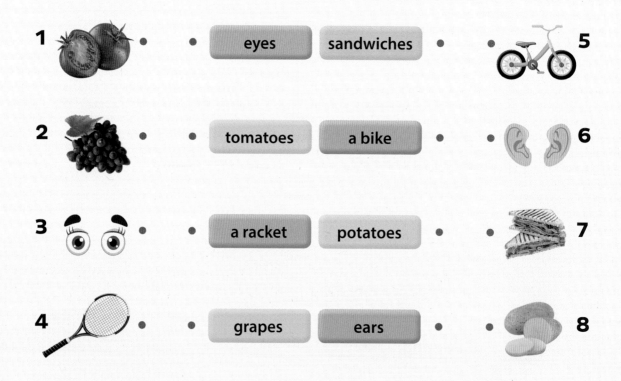

1 • • eyes | sandwiches • • 5

2 • • tomatoes | a bike • • 6

3 • • a racket | potatoes • • 7

4 • • grapes | ears • • 8

B Listen and circle the correct picture.

C Look at the picture. Listen and choose the correct sentence.

1

I like hamburgers.
Do you like hamburgers?

_____.

a   b   c

2

Does she like sweet potatoes?

_____.

a   b   c

3

Do you have a basketball?

_____.

a   b   c

4

Does he have long arms?

_____.

a   b   c

D Listen and number.

E **Talk about the food you like.**

STEP I Choose and write the correct sentence for each blank.

I like tomatoes

I like apples

I don't like donuts

I like apples.
Do you like apples?

Yes. _____.

I like donuts.
What do you like?

_____,
but I like sandwiches.

Do you like vegetables?

Yes. _____.
Do you like tomatoes, too?

No. I don't like tomatoes, but I like tomato ketchup.

STEP 2 Draw the face below to express your likes and dislikes.

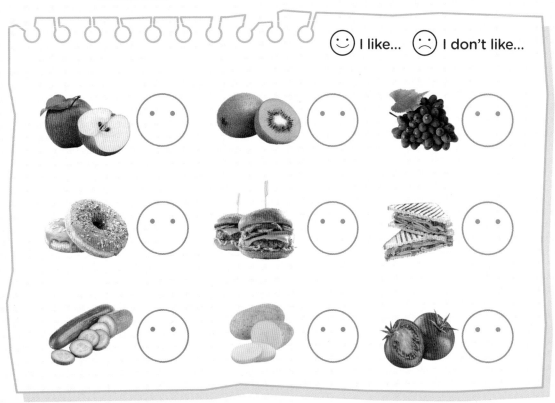

STEP 3 Write about the food you like and don't like. Talk about them with your friends.

I like _____.

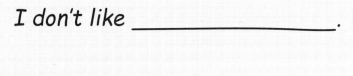

I don't like _____.

Do you like _____?

SCOPE & SEQUENCE

UNIT 01 These are my jeans.

Key Patterns	Vocabulary	Useful Expression	Goals
These are (not) my jeans. Those are (not) my boots.	jeans / socks / boots / glasses / shoes / shorts / pajamas / pants / sandals / sunglasses / earrings / gloves	**Nice boots!** **Useful Questions** Are these your jeans? Are those your boots?	• Identifying objects (clothes & accessories) • Making affirmative/negative statements ● **Theme** Clothes

UNIT 02 I'm eight years old.

Key Patterns	Vocabulary	Useful Expression	Goals
I'm eight years old. She's five years old.	one / two / three / four / five / six / seven / eight / nine / ten / eleven / twelve / thirteen / fourteen / fifteen / sixteen / seventeen / eighteen / nineteen / twenty	**Wacky, this is Amy.** **Useful Question** How old are you?	• Talking about age • Asking and providing answers about a third person's age ● **Theme** Age

UNIT 03 It's cold.

Key Patterns	Vocabulary	Useful Expressions	Goals
Is it cold? It's (not) cold.	windy / sunny / snowy / rainy / foggy / cold / hot / cloudy / stormy / dry / warm / cool	**Excuse me.** **Let's go outside/inside.** **Useful Question** How's the weather?	• Talking about the weather • Making affirmative/negative statements ● **Theme** Weather

UNIT 04 It's in the bag.

Key Patterns	Vocabulary	Useful Expression	Goals
It's in the bag. They're under the bed. They're on your head!	watch / cap / slippers / mittens / in / on / under / belt / umbrella / rain boots / earphones / behind / in front of / next to	**Here they are.** **Useful Questions** Where's my watch? Where are my slippers?	• Talking about positions • Singular/Plural forms ● **Theme** Positions

REVIEW TEST 1 UNIT 01-04

UNIT 05   I like donuts.

Key Patterns	Vocabulary	Useful Expression	Goal
I like donuts. I don't like donuts.	apples / kiwis / grapes / donuts / hamburgers / sandwiches / bananas / oranges / watermelons / ice cream / cheese / pizza	Plug me in, please. **Useful Questions** Do you like donuts? What do you like?	• Talking about the food that Ss like and dislike ⊛ Theme Food / Fruits

UNIT 06   Does she like vegetables?

Key Patterns	Vocabulary	Useful Expression	Goal
Does she like tomatoes? She likes cucumbers. She doesn't like tomatoes.	cucumbers / onions / tomatoes / carrots / potatoes / pumpkins / sweet potatoes / mushrooms / green peas / eggplants / broccoli / cabbages	That's too much! **Useful Question** Does she like vegetables?	• Talking about a third person's likes and dislikes ⊛ Theme Vegetables

UNIT 07   Do you have a bike?

Key Patterns	Vocabulary	Useful Expressions	Goals
Do you have a bike? I have a bike. I don't have a bike.	a bike / a skateboard / a scooter / a soccer ball / a bat / a racket / a baseball / a basketball / a tennis ball / a sled / a snowboard / inline skates / ice skates	Happy birthday. These are for you. **Useful Question** Do you have a skateboard?	• Talking about possessions • Making affirmative/negative statements ⊛ Theme Sports equipment

UNIT 08   He has big ears.

Key Patterns	Vocabulary	Useful Expression	Goals
Does he have big eyes? He has big ears. He doesn't have big eyes.	a nose / a mouth / eyes / ears / hands / feet / hair / a neck / arms / legs / fingers	You're right. **Useful Question** Are you drawing Jack?	• Talking about body parts • Making affirmative/negative statements ⊛ Theme Body parts

REVIEW TEST 2   UNIT 05-08

WORD LIST

A

apples	35
arms	55

B

bananas	37
baseball	49
basketball	49
bat	47
behind	27
belt	27
bike	47
boots	7
broccoli	43

C

cabbages	43
cap	25
carrots	41
cheese	37
cloudy	21
cold	19
cool	21
cucumbers	41

D

donuts	35
dry	21

E

earphones	27
earrings	9
ears	53
eggplants	43
eight	13
eighteen	15
eleven	15
eyes	53

F

feet	53
fifteen	15
fingers	55
five	13
foggy	19
four	13
fourteen	15

G

glasses	7
gloves	9
grapes	35
green peas	43

H

hair	55
hamburgers	35
hands	53
hot	19

I

ice cream	37
ice skates	49
in	25
in front of	27
inline skates	49

J

jeans	7

K

kiwis	35

L

legs	55

Mission Card

This is a backpack.

Mission Card

This is a robot.

Mission Card

This is a desk.

Mission Card

This is a book.

Mission Card

This is a chair.

Mission Card

This is a board.

Mission Card

That's a clock.

Mission Card

That's a crayon.

Mission Card

That's a notebook.

Mission Card

That's a pencil.

Mission Card

That's a ruler.

Mission Card

These are jeans.

Mission Card	Mission Card	Mission Card
 These are socks.	 These are boots.	 These are glasses.
 These are shoes.	 These are shorts.	 Those are pajamas.
 Those are sandals.	 Those are pants.	 Those are sunglasses.
 Those are gloves.	 Those are earrings.	

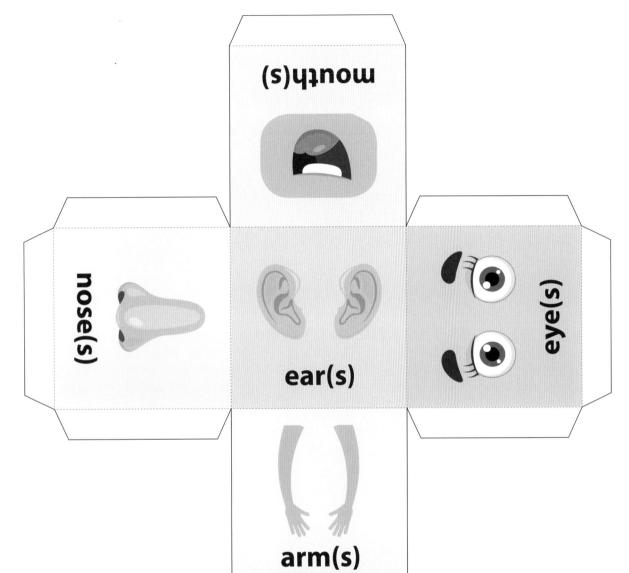

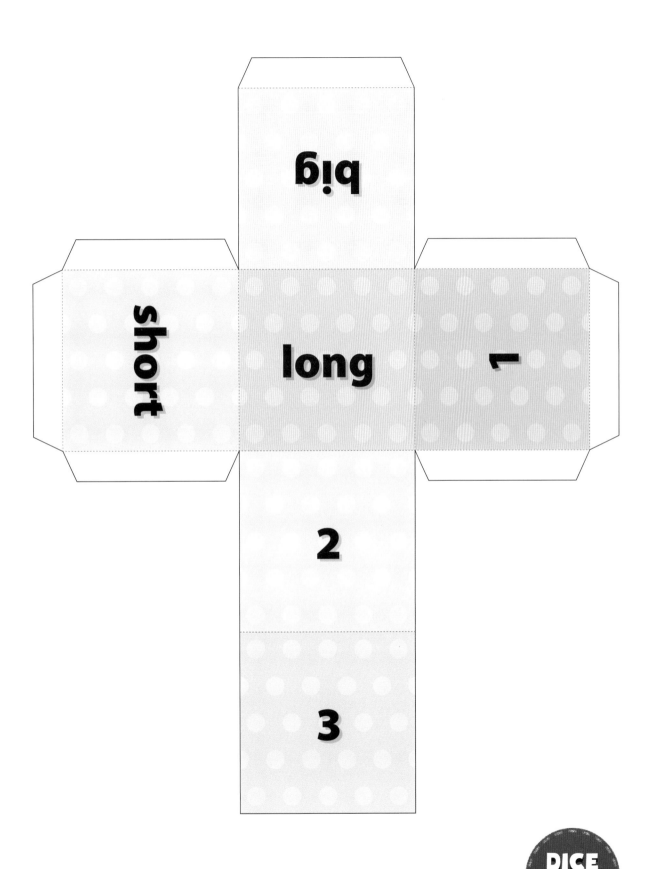

DICE
2

VOCABULARY FLASHCARDS

UNIT 01

UNIT 01

UNIT 01

UNIT 02

UNIT 01

UNIT 01

UNIT 01

UNIT 02

UNIT 01

UNIT 01

UNIT 01

UNIT 02

UNIT 01

UNIT 01

UNIT 01

UNIT 02

UNIT 02

jeans	socks	boots	glasses
shoes	shorts	sunglasses	earrings
gloves	pajamas	pants	sandals
one	two	three	four

UNIT 02

17

UNIT 02

13

UNIT 02

9

UNIT 02

5

UNIT 02

18

UNIT 02

14

UNIT 02

10

UNIT 02

6

UNIT 02

19

UNIT 02

15

UNIT 02

11

UNIT 02

7

UNIT 02

20

UNIT 02

16

UNIT 02

12

UNIT 02

8

five	six	seven	eight
nine	ten	eleven	twelve
thirteen	fourteen	fifteen	sixteen
seventeen	eighteen	nineteen	twenty

UNIT 04

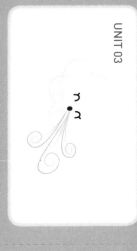

UNIT 03

UNIT 03

UNIT 03

UNIT 04

UNIT 03

UNIT 03

UNIT 03

UNIT 04

UNIT 03

UNIT 03

UNIT 03

UNIT 04

UNIT 03

UNIT 03

UNIT 03

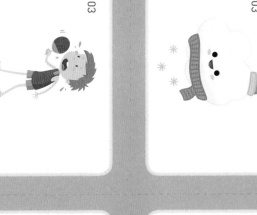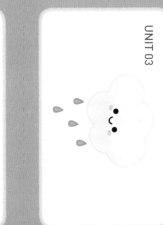

windy	sunny	snowy	rainy
foggy	cold	hot	cloudy
stormy	dry	warm	cool
watch	cap	slippers	mittens

VOCABULARY FLASHCARDS

UNIT 04

UNIT 04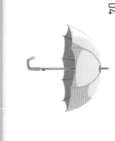

UNIT 05

UNIT 04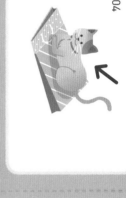

UNIT 04

UNIT 04

UNIT 05

UNIT 04

UNIT 04

UNIT 05

UNIT 05

UNIT 04

UNIT 04

UNIT 05

UNIT 05

UNIT 05

in

umbrella

in front of

grapes

on

rain boots

next to

donuts

under

earphones

apples

hamburgers

belt

behind

kiwis

sandwiches

VOCABULARY FLASHCARDS

UNIT 05

UNIT 05

UNIT 06

UNIT 06

UNIT 05

UNIT 05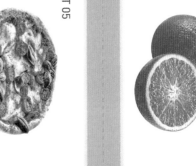

UNIT 06

UNIT 06

UNIT 05

UNIT 06

UNIT 06

UNIT 06

UNIT 05

UNIT 06

UNIT 06

UNIT 06

ice cream	watermelons	oranges	bananas
onions	cucumbers	pizza	cheese
pumpkins	potatoes	carrots	tomatoes
eggplants	green peas	mushrooms	sweet potatoes

UNIT 06

UNIT 07

UNIT 07

UNIT 07

UNIT 06

UNIT 07

UNIT 07

UNIT 07

UNIT 07

UNIT 07

UNIT 07

UNIT 07

UNIT 07

UNIT 07

UNIT 07

UNIT 08

broccoli	cabbages	a bike	a skateboard
a scooter	a soccer ball	a bat	a racket
a baseball	a basketball	a tennis ball	a sled
a snowboard	inline skates	ice skates	a nose

UNIT 08

UNIT 08

UNIT 08

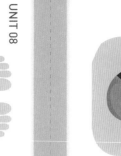

UNIT 08

UNIT 08

UNIT 08

UNIT 08

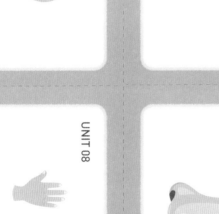

UNIT 08

UNIT 08

UNIT 08

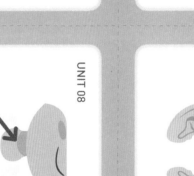

UNIT 08

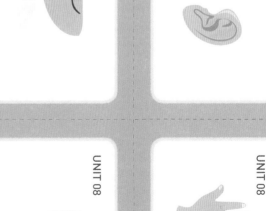

UNIT 08

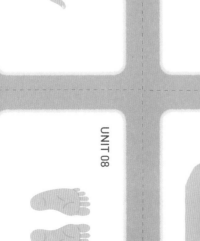

UNIT 08

UNIT 08

UNIT 08

UNIT 08

a mouth	feet	legs	big eyes
eyes	hair	fingers	small ears
ears	a neck	a big nose	small hands
hands	arms	a big mouth	small feet

UNIT 08

UNIT 08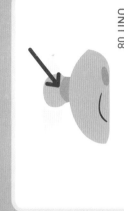

UNIT 08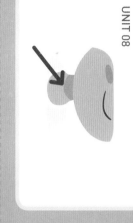

UNIT 08

UNIT 08

short hair

long fingers

a short neck

long arms

long legs

UNIT 01

These are my

UNIT 01

Those are my

UNIT 02

I'm

UNIT 02

She's

UNIT 01

These are not my

UNIT 01

Those are not my

UNIT 02

He's

UNIT 02

year(s) old

UNIT 02

year(s) old

UNIT 03

Is it

UNIT 03

It's not

UNIT 04

It's on

UNIT 02

year(s) old

UNIT 03

It's

UNIT 04

It's in

UNIT 04

It's under

UNIT 04

They're in

UNIT 04

They're under

UNIT 04

It's in front of

UNIT 04

They're behind

UNIT 04

They're on

UNIT 04

It's behind

UNIT 04

It's next to

UNIT 04

They're in front of

UNIT 04

They're next to

UNIT 05

I don't like

UNIT 06

Does she like

UNIT 06

She likes

UNIT 05

I like

UNIT 06

Does he like

UNIT 06

He likes

UNIT 06

He doesn't like

UNIT 06

She doesn't like

UNIT 07

I have

UNIT 08

Does he have

UNIT 08

He has

UNIT 07

Do you have

UNIT 07

I don't have

UNIT 08

Does she have

UNIT 08

She has

UNIT 08

He doesn't have

UNIT 08

She doesn't have

?

·

·

?

·

·

1 구문

판매 1위 '천일문' 콘텐츠를 활용하여 정확하고 다양한 구문 학습

끊어읽기　　해석하기　　문장 구조 분석　　해설·해석 제공　　단어 스크램블링　　영작하기

2 문법·서술형

쎄듀의 모든 문법 문항을 활용하여 내신까지 해결하는 정교한 문법 유형 제공

객관식과 주관식의 결합　　문법 포인트별 학습　　보기를 활용한 집합 문항　　내신대비 서술형　　어법+서술형 문제

3 어휘

초·중·고·공무원까지 방대한 어휘량을 제공하며 오프라인 TEST 인쇄도 가능

영단어 카드 학습　　단어 ↔ 뜻 유형　　예문 활용 유형　　단어 매칭 게임

4 선생님 보유 문항 이용

Online Test　　OMR Test

☕ cafe.naver.com/cedulearnteacher

쎄듀런 학습 정보가 궁금하다면?

쎄듀런 Cafe

· 쎄듀런 사용법 안내 & 학습법 공유
· 공지 및 문의사항 QA
· 할인 쿠폰 증정 등 이벤트 진행

with 세이펜

원어민 음성을 실시간 반복학습	단어 및 대화의 우리말 해석 듣기	선생님의 Workbook Guide로 혼자서도 쉽게 학습

세이펜 핀파일 다운로드 안내

STEP ① 세이펜과 컴퓨터를 USB 케이블로 연결하세요.

STEP ② 쎄듀북 홈페이지(www.cedubook.com)에 접속 후, 학습자료실 메뉴에서 학습할 교재를 찾아 이동합니다.

> 초등교재 ▶ ELT ▶ 학습교재 클릭 ▶ 세이펜 핀파일 자료 클릭
> ▶ 다운로드 (저장을 '다른 이름으로 저장'으로 변경하여 저장소를 USB로 변경) ▶ 완료

STEP ③ 음원 다운로드가 완료되면 세이펜과 컴퓨터의 USB 케이블을 분리하세요.

STEP ④ 세이펜을 분리하면 "시스템을 초기화 중입니다. 잠시만 기다려 주세요." 라는 멘트가 나옵니다.

STEP ⑤ 멘트 종료 후 세이펜을 〈Oh! My Speaking〉 표지에 대보세요.
효과음이 나온 후 바로 학습을 시작할 수 있습니다.

참고사항

◆ 세이펜은 본 교재에 포함되어 있지 않습니다. 별도로 구매하여 이용할 수 있으며, 기존에 보유하신 세이펜이 있다면 핀파일만 다운로드해서
　바로 이용하실 수 있습니다.

◆ 세이펜에서 제작된 모든 기종(기존에 보유하고 계신 기종도 호환 가능)으로 사용이 가능합니다.

◆ 모든 기종은 세이펜에서 권장하는 최신 펌웨어 업데이트를 진행해 주시기 바랍니다.
　업데이트는 세이펜 홈페이지(www.saypen.com)에서 가능합니다.

◆ 핀파일은 쎄듀북 홈페이지(www.cedubook.com)와 세이펜 홈페이지(www.saypen.com)에서 모두 다운로드 가능합니다.

◆ 세이펜을 이용하지 않는 학습자는 쎄듀북 홈페이지 부가학습자료, 교재 내 QR코드 이미지 등을 활용하여 원어민 음성으로 학습하실 수 있습니다.

◆ 기타 문의사항은 www.cedubook.com / 02-3272-4766으로 연락 바랍니다.

Oh! MY SPEAKING

2

with SAYPEN

MP3 CD Included

SAYPEN TV
www.saypen.com

CEDU BOOK

Oh! my SPEAKING 2

WORKBOOK

CEDU BOOK

UNIT 01 These are my jeans.

A Unscramble the words.

HELP

1

t o b
o s

_____

2

e j a
s n

_____

3

a s s
g l s e

_____

4

c o
s k s

_____

B Look and write.

HELP

1

These are my _____ .

2

Those are not _____ .

Those are my _____ .

C **Trace and write.**

HELP

gloves   pants   glasses   shoes   earrings

1

Are these your _____?

Yes. These are my _____.

2

Are those your _____?

Yes. Those are my _____.

3

Are these your glasses?

No. These are not _____.

These are my _____.

4

Are those your _____?

Yes. Those are my _____.

D Listen and number.

E Listen and choose the right sentence for the blank.

1

 Are these your pajamas?

 a   b   c   _____.

2

 Are those your sunglasses?

 a   b   c   _____.

F Choose the right answer for the blank.

HELP

a Those are not my boots

b These are my jeans

c These are my socks

YOUR TURN! Choose one item and complete the sentence.

These are my _____.

UNIT 02   I'm eight years old.

A **Count, match, and unscramble the words.**

HELP

1   ● ●   ●   ● n e o   _____

2   ● ● ● ●   ●   ● e h t i g   _____

3   ● ● ● ● ● ●   ●   ● x i s   _____

4   ● ● ● ● ● ● ● ●   ●   ● t e h r e   _____

B **Look and write.**

HELP

1   7   I'm _____ years old.

2   5   He's _____ years old.

C **Trace and write.**

HELP

| two | nine | four | ten |

1

How old are you?

I'm _____ years old.

2

How old is she?

She's _____ years old.

3

How old are you?

I'm _____ years old.

4

How old is he?

He's _____ years old.

D Listen and choose the right picture.

67
HELP

1

2

3

4

E Listen and choose the right sentence for the blank.

68
HELP

1

How old are you?

ⓐ ⓑ ⓒ

2

How old is he?

ⓐ ⓑ ⓒ

F Choose the right answer for the blank.

HELP

Wacky, this is Amy. Amy, this is Wacky.

Nice to meet you.

Nice to meet you, too.

I'm eight years old. How old are you, Amy?

_____, too. Wacky, how old are you?

_____.

This is my little sister. _____.

Oh, you're a baby.

No! I'm not a baby. I'm a robot.

a She's five years old   **b** I'm one year old

c I'm eight years old

YOUR TURN! Draw one of your family members and write.

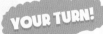

This is my _____.

He's/She's _____ years old.

UNIT 03 It's cold.

A Complete the puzzle.

HELP

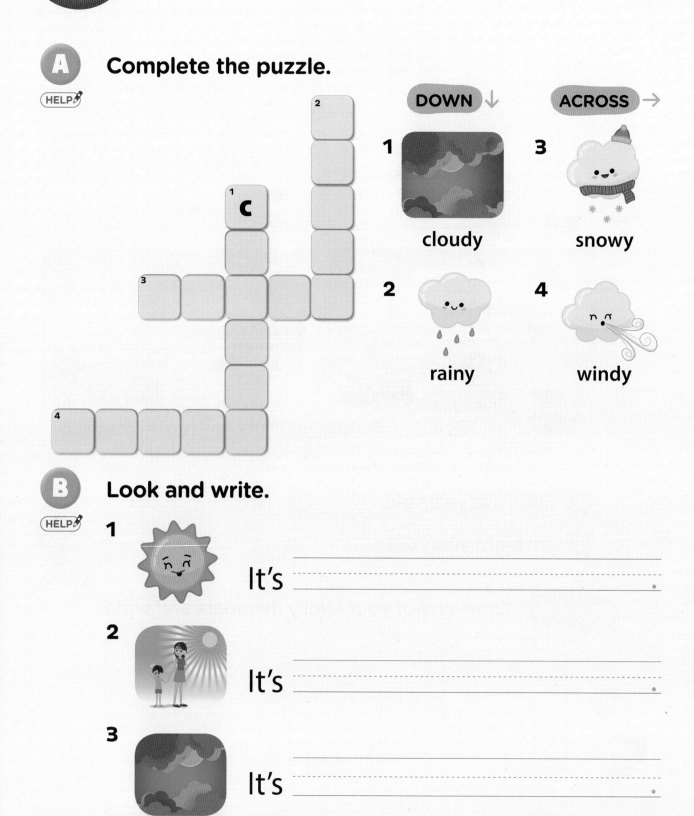

DOWN ↓

1 cloudy

2 rainy

ACROSS →

3 snowy

4 windy

B Look and write.

HELP

1 It's _____.

2 It's _____.

3 It's _____.

C Trace and write.

HELP

| snowy | foggy | stormy | cloudy | cold |

1

Is it _____ ?

Yes. It's _____ .

2

Is it _____ ?

Yes. It's _____ .

3

Is it _____ ?

Yes. It's _____ .

4

Is it foggy? _____

No. It's not _____ .

It's _____ .

D Listen and choose the right picture.

1

2

3

4

E Listen and choose the right sentence for the blank.

1

 How's the weather? Is it dry?

 a b c _____.

2

 Is it windy?

 a b c _____.

Choose the right answer for the blank.

HELP

How's the weather?

_____.

_____?

No. It's not cold.

Look! There's Amy.

Let's go outside.

Achoo! Excuse me.

Sorry! _____.
Let's go inside.

a It's so cold

b Is it cold

c It's windy

YOUR TURN! **Draw today's weather and write about it.**

It's _____.

It's in the bag.

 A Match and fill in the blanks.

1  • • __ a t __ __

2 • • __ a __

3  • • __ __ i p __ e r s

4 • • __ e l __

 B Where is the watch? Look and write.

1 It's _____ the bag.

2 It's _____ the bag.

3 They're _____ the bag.

C Trace and write.

HELP

belt	umbrella	watch	mittens
under	in front of	on	next to

1

Where's my _____?

It's _____ the desk.

2

Where's my _____?

It's _____ the desk.

3

Where's my _____?

It's _____ the bag.

4

Where are my _____?

They're _____ the bag.

D Listen and number.

71
HELP

E Listen and choose the right sentence for the blank.

72
HELP

1

Where's my umbrella?

_____

2

Where are my rain boots?

_____

F Choose the right answer for the blank.

HELP

Where's my watch?

Where are my slippers?

Oh, here they are. Thanks, Wacky.

You're welcome.

Where are my sunglasses? They're not in the bag.

a It's in the bag

b They're on your head

c They're under the bed

YOUR TURN! Draw one item with the bag and complete the sentences.

Where's my _____?

It's _____ the bag.

UNIT 05 I like donuts.

A Unscramble the words.

HELP

1

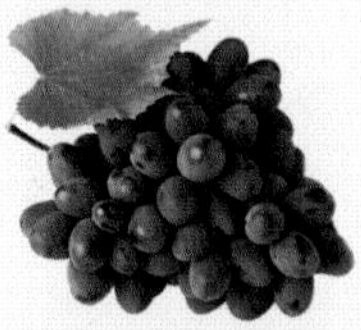

r g a
s e p

2

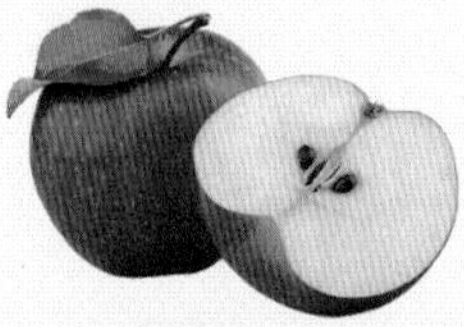

a p e
s p l

3

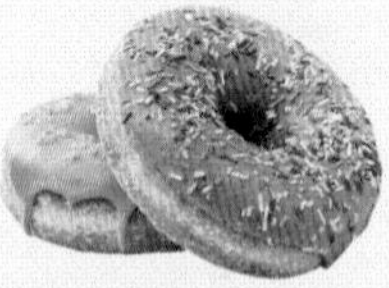

n o u
t d s

4

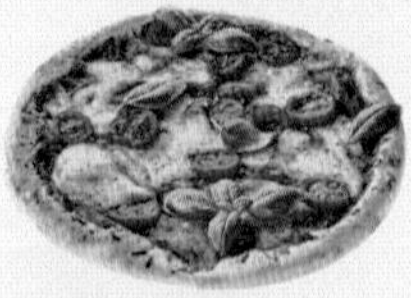

i z
p z a

B Look and write.

HELP

1

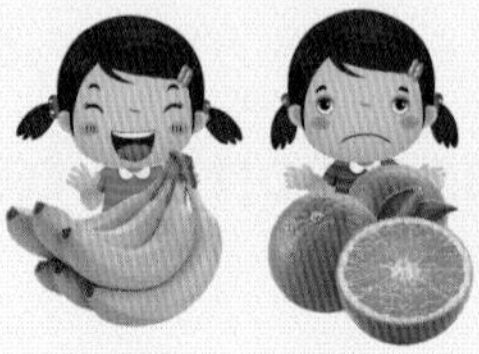

I like ______________________.

I don't like ______________________.

2

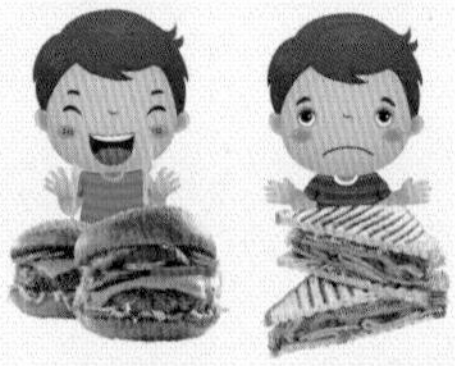

I like ______________________.

I don't like ______________________.

Trace and write.

HELP

| donuts | watermelons | ice cream | pizza | kiwis |

1

Do you like ?

Yes. I like .

2

Do you like ?

No. I don't like .

3

Do you like ?

Yes. I like .

4

Do you like donuts?

No. I don't like .

I like .

D Listen and draw the face below the food.

☺ I like...   ☹ I don't like...

1

2

3

4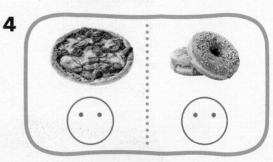

E Listen and choose the right sentence for the blank.

1

Do you like ice cream?

    _____.

2

I like oranges.
Do you like oranges?

    _____.

HELP

F Choose the right answer for the blank.

I like donuts.
Do you like donuts?

No. _____.

_____.
Do you like kiwis?

No. _____ kiwis.

Then what do you like?

Well…

I don't like food.
I don't eat food.
Plug me in, please.

Oh, I see. Okay!

a I don't like donuts

b I don't like

c I like kiwis

YOUR TURN! Choose an item and complete the sentences.

☺ I like _____ .

☹ I don't like _____ .

Does she like tomatoes?

A Unscramble the words and match.

1 u m b e
c u c r s

_____

2 a o r c
r t s

_____

3 t a t e
s o m o

_____

4 n s o
i o n

_____

B Look and write.

1  She likes _____

She doesn't like _____

2 He likes _____

He doesn't like _____

C **Trace and write.**

potatoes	onions	pumpkins
green peas	mushrooms	cucumbers

1

Does she like _____?

Yes. She likes _____.

2

Does she like onions?

No. She doesn't like _____.

She likes _____.

3

Does he like _____?

Yes. He likes _____.

4

Does he like green peas?

No. He doesn't like _____.

He likes _____.

D Listen and number.

E Listen and choose the right sentence for the blank.

1

 Does he like broccoli?

2

 Does she like onions?

F Choose the right answer for the blank.

Let's make breakfast for Mom.

Okay.

_____ vegetables?

Yes. _____ and potatoes.

I see. Does she like tomatoes?

No. _____ tomatoes, but she likes tomato ketchup.

Okay. Let's put in tomato ketchup.

Oh no! That's too much!

 **a** Does she like

b She doesn't like

c She likes cucumbers

YOUR TURN! Ask your friend what vegetables he/she likes or doesn't like. Then write.

My friend's name:

He/She likes _____ .

He/She doesn't like _____ .

UNIT 07 Do you have a bike?

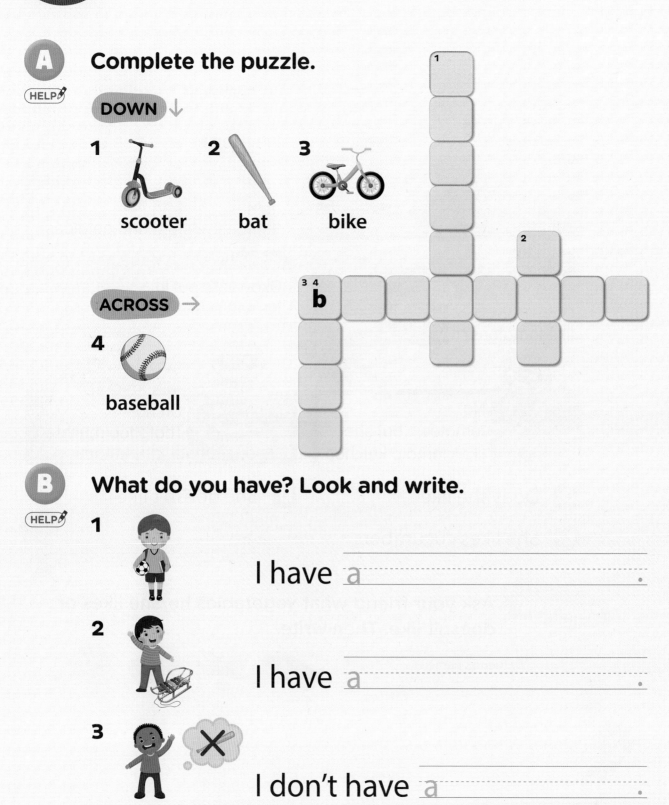

A Complete the puzzle.

HELP

DOWN ↓

1 scooter

2 bat

3 bike

ACROSS →

4 baseball

B What do you have? Look and write.

HELP

1 I have a _____ .

2 I have a _____ .

3 I don't have a _____ .

C Trace and write.

a tennis ball   inline skates

a snowboard   a basketball   a racket

1

Do you have   ?

Yes. I have   .

2

Do you have   ?

Yes. I have   .

3

Do you have   ?

Yes. I have   .

4

Do you have a racket?

No. I don't have   .

I have   .

D Listen and choose the right picture.

1 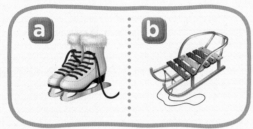 **2**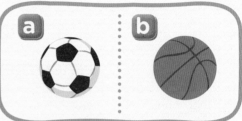

3  **4**

E Listen and choose the right sentence for the blank.

1

Do you have ice skates?

a b c _____.

2

Do you have a bat?

a b c _____.

F Choose the right answer for the blank.

HELP

Do you have a bike?

Yes. _____.

No. I don't have a bike.

_____?

Yes. I have a skateboard.

No. _____.

Happy birthday, Wacky! These are for you.

Wow!

Now I have a skateboard. Thank you.

Great!

a I don't have a skateboard   **b** I have a bike

c Do you have a skateboard

 **YOUR TURN!** Choose an item and complete the sentences.

I have _____.

I don't have _____.

UNIT 08 He has big ears.

A Match and fill in the blanks.

HELP

1 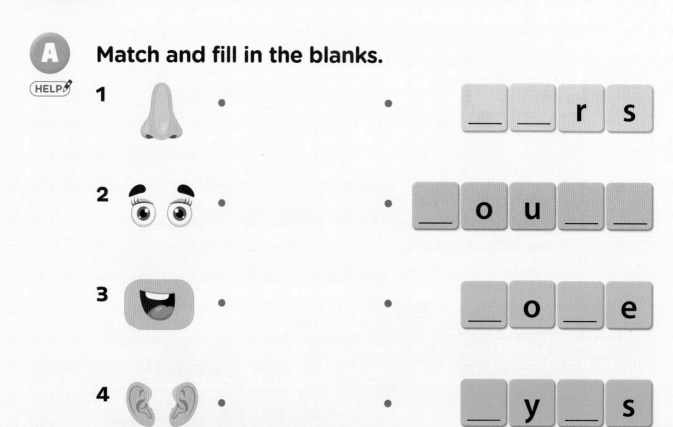 • • __ __ r s

2 • • __ o u __ __

3 • • __ o __ e

4 • • __ y __ s

B Look and write.

HELP

1  She doesn't have small _____ .

She has big _____ .

2  He doesn't have a long _____ .

He has a short _____ .

C Trace and write.

HELP

| fingers | neck | feet | legs |

1 Does she have a long neck?

No. She doesn't have

a long .

She has a short .

2 Does she have long ?

Yes. She has long .

3 Does he have big ?

Yes. He has big .

4 Does he have short fingers?

No. He doesn't have

short .

He has long .

D Listen and number.

HELP

E Listen and choose the right sentence for the blank.

HELP

1

Does he have a small nose?

_____.

2

Does she have a short neck?

_____.

F Choose the right answer for the blank.

HELP

Are you drawing Jack?

Does he have big eyes?

Yes. Jack has big ears.

You're right. _____.

No. _____.
He has small eyes.

He has a long tail.

What? I don't have a tail!

It's a cat.

He doesn't have a tail!

_____ a long tail.

a She has

b He doesn't have big eyes

c He has big ears

YOUR TURN! Describe the monster.

He has big _____.

He has long _____.

He doesn't have _____.

WORKBOOK GUIDE

(HELP)

- Try to do the workbook activities on your own as much as possible.
- If you need additional help or want to hear the answers, scan the appropriate QR code below using your phone.
- You will be able to listen to the teacher's explanation immediately!

UNIT 01

A   B   C   D   E   F

UNIT 02

A   B   C   D   E   F

UNIT 03

A   B   C   D   E   F

UNIT 04

A   B   C   D   E   F

UNIT 05

A   B   C   D   E   F

UNIT 06

A   B   C   D   E   F

UNIT 07

A   B   C   D   E   F

UNIT 08

A   B   C   D   E   F

Oh! My Speaking is a six-level speaking series designed for young learners. With task-based activities and vivid illustrations, *Oh! My Speaking* allows students to build up their confidence in speaking and to communicate with their peers in fun and interesting ways. By focusing on basic key words and key patterns with *Oh! My Speaking*, students set out on the journey toward becoming strong speakers of English.

Oh! My Speaking Series

SAYCODE II
SAYPEN
Oh! My Speaking
SD4-OHMS

세이펜과 함께 배우는 Oh! My Speaking

〈Oh! My Speaking〉은 세이펜이 적용된 도서입니다. 세이펜을 가져다 대면 원어민의 생생한 영어 발음과 억양을 듣고 영어 말하기 연습을 할 수 있습니다.

***번역 기능** | 세이펜으로 책을 찍어서 원어민 음성을 들은 후, T 버튼을 짧게 누르면 우리말 해석 음원을 들을 수 있습니다.

✏ 세이펜을 대면 유닛명을 들을 수 있습니다. T 기능 지원

✏ QR코드에 세이펜을 대면 해당 MP3파일이 재생됩니다.

✏ 세이펜을 대면 Activity의 지시문을 들을 수 있습니다. T 기능 지원

✏ 그림이나 영어 단어에 세이펜을 대면 원어민의 발음을 들을 수 있습니다. T 기능 지원

✏ 그림이나 영어 단어에 세이펜을 대면 원어민의 발음을 들을 수 있습니다. T 기능 지원

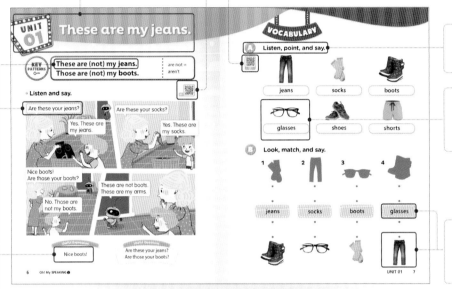

✏ 영어 문장에 세이펜을 대면 원어민의 정확한 발음과 억양을 들을 수 있습니다. T 기능 지원

✏ 번호에 세이펜을 대면 해당 그림에 대한 Key Pattern 대화가 재생되며, 그림이나 영어 단어에 세이펜을 대면 해당하는 영어 단어를 들을 수 있습니다. T 기능 지원

✏ 영어 문장이나 단어에 세이펜을 대면 원어민의 정확한 발음과 억양을 들을 수 있습니다. T 기능 지원

✏ 그림에 세이펜을 대면 해당 그림에 대한 Key Pattern 대화를 들을 수 있습니다. T 기능 지원

✏ 문제 번호나 그림에 세이펜을 대면 해당 문제의 음원이 재생되며, 영어 문장에 세이펜을 대면 해당 문장 또는 정답 영어 문장을 들을 수 있습니다. T 기능 지원

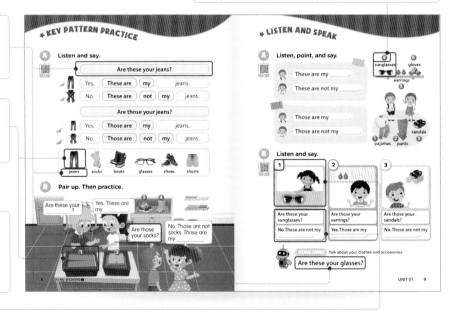

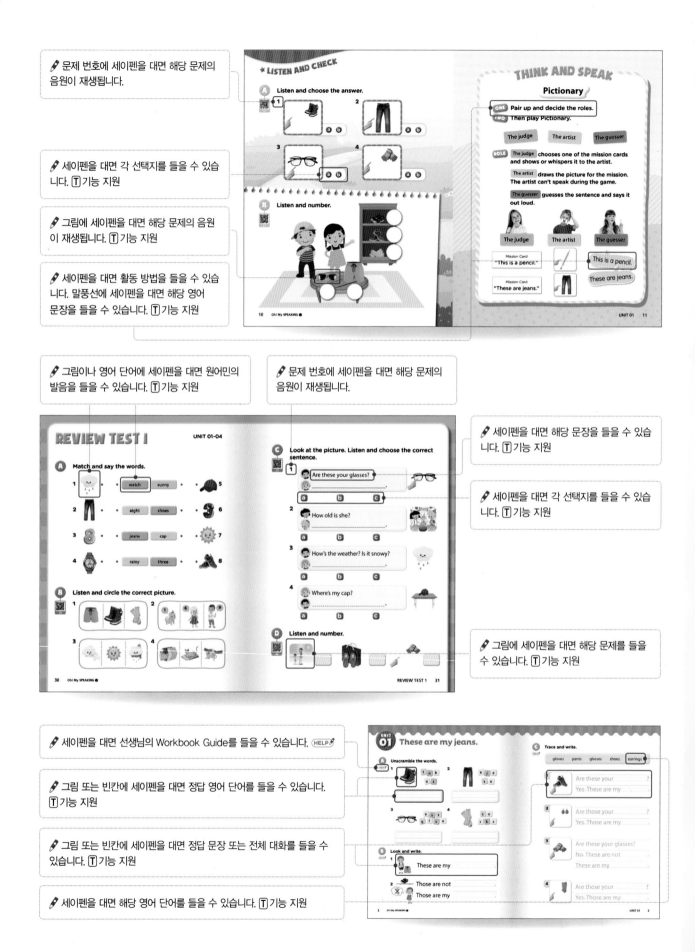